swell

Christopher Lanyon is a poet and mathematician from Cornwall. This is his first pamphlet of poetry.

swell

Published by Bad Betty Press in 2022
www.badbettypress.com

All rights reserved

Christopher Lanyon has asserted his right to be identified as the author of this work in accordance with Section 77 of the Copyright, Designs and Patents Act of 1988.

Cover illustration by Nicola Toon

Printed and bound in the United Kingdom

A CIP record of this book is available from the British Library.

ISBN: 978-1-913268-26-8

SWELL

For Mum, who keeps asking when I'll write a poem about her, even though she's read the ones I wrote about Dad.

BAD BETTY
PRESS

Contents

Poachers	7
Peel out	8
Poem for Huers	9
Years after the car crash	10
Pitch	12
Lockets are a terrible metaphor for chest pain because they mostly hurt my fingernails when I cannot get them open	13
Do not forget my name. Do not forget me.	14
Hen	15
Figures in a Landscape	16
Praa Sands	18
Stop calling birds by their Latin names;	19
Portrait of my dad as a woodsman	20
Calgary	21
Bathers	22
Ars Poetica with Dad	23
Pamphlet I have not written about my grandad	24
Sugar loaf	26
Gannets	27
Acknowledgements	32

Poachers
After Han Kang

Did your father feel a lightness in his breast when I,
pray-he-is-never-son-in-law boy, left? He stared
at my bird of paradise chest, had to put the TV on mute
to be sure that we fucked like wood pigeons. At
night we would sneak down to the swift estuary, to pick the
plump oysters and peck salt off each other's bodies. A flame's
flickering light lit your parents' faces; I watched your mother wavering.
The froth and spittle on your father's lips drew the outline
of a man more preacher than English teacher. His fluttering
heart thrummed a prayer for escape and his veins popped blue like
the springtime forest floor. I watched your mother, trembling. A
bas-relief of father's rage now playing on her features, a bird's
call ringing in the hollow parts of her. The rest left translucent,
her hand on his shoulder as light as a broken wing.

Peel out

I've been eating a bag of clementines a day. I googled *how many oranges do you have to eat a day before it kills you* feeling ambivalent about the answer. One of the things worth living for is eating a bag of clementines a day. I leave a fine spray of sticky juice across my computer screen. My nails and fingertips are turning that sickly nicotine yellow that boys love to write about but this time it's not cigarettes, it's eating a bag of clementines a day. This is the kind of shit where people say *well if that's your only vice*—but it isn't my only vice I also like cigarettes and tequila and videogames and sex and impressing people who give tours of breweries with my superior knowledge of yeast and worrying about my receding hairline and drinking sparkling water by the two-litre bottle until I piss every fifteen minutes. But I'm not eating a bag of any of those a day. I'm eating a bag of clementines a day.

Poem for Huers

My dad drew a knife down the seam of fish belly,
spilling bitter innards over his hands and thighs.
He picked through a prophecy of yellow-fin guts.

In Cornwall they would have hollered *heva* from the clifftops—
the darkness of a bait-ball, ink blotting the granite swell.

Each fish is a tensing muscle,
whipping against the indignity of beaching.

Each fish is a feast in waiting,
a slab of quartz-flesh and hard scales,
iridescent on the flat bottom of a porcelain sink.

My dad drew the knife down the seam: spilling butter-
glossy offal, the others could not watch.

Years after the car crash

Emma tagged me and 24 friends
in an advert for knockoff Ray Bans;

whoever hacked her Facebook
doesn't know that she is dead.

The last time we were together
we fell asleep stoned on the sofa

of her terraced student house.
We were secretly holding hands.

I didn't tell my girlfriend;
I didn't want it to mean something.

Before then we had kissed in stairwells,
wandered drunk through Brandon Hill.

We were always trying to prove
how impossible it was to die.

At the funeral the priest
called Emma an undying servant

of God. But we knew her cider-lipped
and happy, brilliant, gorse fire

on the Welsh hills. I hated everyone
in the church for their refusal to say

who she really was, for calling her
undying when she was so clearly dead.

I wondered if the man in a cast
was the driver of the other car.

We skipped out on the wake
and went to a Wetherspoons.

I thought I saw her there at a high table:
a smile; a full glass, raised.

I did not know how to say goodbye.

Pitch
After Charles Wright

Standing with my back to the wall, goalposts drawn on
in chalk. Knees bent, palms open—ready for the slap,
the prickling skin, a small victory. Jordan yells
he's only good in goal if you kick it straight at him.

I want to be as beautiful as a flooded quarry
I want to be quick, swifter than the turn of a roebuck's head
I want to be strong, muscular, blooming
I want to be bruised and told that I am brave

And every mouth will open to scream my name
And they will carry me on their shoulders like they carry hurt
And we will win but I will never get better
And the locker room walls will crumble, until we see the sky

Lockets are a terrible metaphor for chest pain because they mostly hurt my fingernails when I cannot get them open

My mother broke a kaleidoscope over her knee
to prove there was nothing special about beautiful things

her knee was a cascade of scarab beetle & harlequin & fool's gold
my knee was a cascade of cochineal / of red dye number 4

when she told me I was brave / when she told me I was special
I knew I was not a beautiful thing but maybe a knife mark

or the ringing of bells in my father's hands / in the churches the positions
of bellringer and pallbearer often conflict because both require strong arms

strong arms are not special but they are a beautiful thing
my father carries a rope on his shoulder and his vowels smell like coffee

he has shortened me to consonants now that I am taller than him
his cheeks a cascade of hissing cockroaches

please sing in unison I/he/my mother/I whisper please ring
pizzicato/leave breaks between notes so that I can hear the

hurt/hertz

Do not forget my name. Do not forget me.

On Christmas Day we watch Les Misérables. Everyone thinks Russell Crowe was poorly cast except me. Grandad thinks you shouldn't make a musical if you refuse to be historically accurate. We fight about it. Russell has been bloviating and talk-singing for what feels like hours. He finally realises that morality isn't cut and dry, that people are capable of nuance and goodness and change. Then he throws himself off the bridge. The room is lousy with the crunch of Russell Crowe's bones. Then quiet. All of us pray that Grandad has fallen asleep, that his face is not folding into tears. That he has not been visited, once again, by his son's falling body.

Hen

I think about flightless birds the most.
Their sometimes-strong legs.
Or the wingspan of a chicken, spread
like a halfhearted promise.

My grandad kept chickens. He named them
and ate their eggs. He loved them
until one after the other they were foxed
out of the coop. Another period of mourning.

Springtime frost silvered the ground.
The dead grass grew back until
he could remember a life without them
or he could not remember them at all.

Figures in a Landscape

Barbara Hepworth invented negative space.
Her sculpture Pelagos is as tight and hollow as the wind over St Ives Bay.
In gallery four a woman asks me to approve her nudes
before she sends them to a stranger.

Wonders *do you ever think about sinkholes?*
They are my favourite kind of natural disaster.
I tell her I have started dreaming about tidal waves crashing
against the curved feature window of gallery two, trying to break in.

Tourists ask *where's the real art?*

Barbara Hepworth used to lock her assistants in her workshop
to hide them from visitors. Once, Terry Frost was alone in there so long
he pissed on the floor like a panicked dog.
That night, when the guests had left,
Hepworth fucked Ben Nicholson's brains out with a chisel
pressed to his breastbone.

I am sick of telling people what they cannot do.

A child runs a finger along the curve of Pelagos.
A woman cups the bronze breasts of The Swimmer.
A security guard puts his boot on a priceless slab of plexiglass,
casting ripples onto the wall of gallery one.

The curved feature window of gallery two is a portrait of the sea.
The sea is not white horses and saltwater it is a tide
of oily fingers of grasping hands.
The sea is being permanently plagiarised.

A feedback form calls the building a brutal act
of architectural masturbation.

The gallery assistants gather in quiet corners and talk about bad dreams.
A high wind. A hang glider. The cold heart of a mine shaft. Barbara
Hepworth.				Barbara
Hepworth.				Barbara
Hepworth.				Barbara
Hepworth's ghost in the sea fret, on the cliffs.

Tourists ask *where's the real art?*

I tell them that Barbara Hepworth dropped a cigarette
in her sleep and burned it all down
before the sea could take it back.

Praa Sands

And then there was my best friend's body:
broader, and hairy in a way I had not noticed before.
And me in bed waiting for him to strip down to his boxers.
Both of us fresh out of the shower, drunk still.
I took him in my arms and joked a kiss onto his shoulder.
He shrank inwards like a sea anemone
prodded by the guileless finger of a tourist.
He told me that Maddie was the only person
to ever spoon him and he could not bear it.
I rolled away and thought about the glow-in-the-dark stars
my parents had scattered across my bedroom ceiling,
how much barer this ceiling was without them.
Luke lay on his side, a body of jutting Cornish rock,
forming a bay in the sheets between us.
And the sea was spread out
like it had been earlier that night,
as we stripped down to our boxers
and ran towards the waves, pressing
our thighs into the oncoming water,
cleaving through to find it constellated
with bioluminescent water bugs.
The nighttime sea was dense with them,
but each time we tried to catch one it flickered out
in our palms. The ocean rippled out from us
like the surface of the bed we shared.
We were a quiet coastline, holding something
unspoken between us, unwilling to let it go.

Stop calling birds by their Latin names;

naming a bird won't stop it from dying out. I am trying to write poems about standard-winged nightjars (*Caprimulgus longipennis*) but birds aren't a metaphor for everything. Writing about birds is no way to show love. Not when your love language is a curt nod of the head, a father on the telly, proud of his son. Standard-winged nightjars are not named so because their wings are normal compared to other nightjars, but because they call out to each other by raising and lowering two footlong quills, tipped with broad feathers.

Portrait of my dad as a woodsman
After Bob Hicok

My dad has read every poem I've written about him.
He's spread them out over his desk like wolf guts
on an old woman's bed sheets, found them full
of bruised shins and growing pains and hoods
pulled down hard against driving Cornish rain.
The poems are never about the gentle way he loves the forest
or the timber hitch of muscle in his shoulder blades.
My dad wonders why, in my poems about him,
he's never waving hello from a hilltop at dusk.
He wonders why I've made him a beast of burden:
a man weighed down by the word *father*, a man
with bark-hardened hands, rather than the soft ones
he used to raise me. My dad wonders when my teeth got so big.

Calgary

Dusk has peeled away from the mountains;
roadside trees needle at the settling dark.
Alpine larch, white spruce, quaking aspen.

Kaci lost their footing on a gravel scramble
and fell down the mountainside, skidding
to a stop in the shale and short grass.

Everything in Canada is trying to kill us:
coyotes prowl in the scrublands; truck drivers
keep hunting knives in their glove compartments;

an unclean plate will draw a bear to your campsite;
the hot top of an oil lantern might burn off your fingertips.
This summer a wolf dragged a man out of his tent by the arm.

We are driving home from the hospital.
Kaci is picking grit out of small holes in their legs and chest;
I imagine collapsing into the arms of a smiling paramedic.

The truck ahead of us brakes hard, shudders like a sob
caught in the throat. A deer drags itself onto the verge,
broken foreleg swinging. It moves in stop motion.

Bathers

I can hear you from my room, with two doors and a corridor between us. Muffled, as if it were me sinking into the scald of bathwater, my knees out and cold, my ears sloshing with the breaking waves of your laugh and then theirs. I know how you look undressed: the way purple scars woodlouse across the upturned stones of your shoulder blades. The skin on your chest is as pale as soap suds. When I hear you both singing in the steamy bathroom, naked, pressed against each other, cupped in each other's hands, the scene is all pinks. Dewy lips and tear ducts and cuticles and blisters raised by the heat of the bathwater. When it goes quiet, I know that you are kissing.

Ars Poetica With Dad

Alright dad

you're in this poem now, and I've dressed you
in a brown t-shirt with *geology rocks* printed on it,
like the one we bought you for your birthday. I'm here too.
It's not our first rodeo. This time I promise I won't make you
a woodsman or a bell-ringer or a dog, and I won't be Jesus Christ
in eyeliner or a fish with its belly split open. I hope, in this poem,
we don't become distant men on Bob Hicok's dusky hills.
I hope this time we can talk.

Maybe you'll say *my best boy* at the seaside of this poem
or sat opposite me in a university town coffee shop. And then
I can concentrate on the alliterative quality of parental love,
all the repeating shapes of it. Maybe I'll tell you that,
despite the other poems, it doesn't really matter that you're terrible
at saying *I love you* at the end of phone calls, not when you do
such a good job of showing it. I'll apologise for never giving you credit,
and for calling you *archetype* rather than *dad*.

I've started telling people that I love you during poetry shows,
that you're a good guy. Middle-aged men confess their regrets
to me, pat my shoulder, linger, pretend I'm their son.
My other dad, Seamus Heaney, wrote his pen into a gun
and shot his father into the past with it. I've made mine
a fence, a polished axe handle, a series of blunt objects.
Maybe now, like Seamus, I can make a shovel of it,
and unearth my dad from the wintry soil.

Pamphlet I have not written about my grandad

Portrait of Grandad asleep, mouth open, grasping the sides
of the hospital bed as if they were the guardrails at the bow
of a ship, knees making a sail of the bedsheets 7

Grandad spends 20 minutes looking at a book of pictures of his
hometown, meticulously, page by page. Then hands it back to
my dad and says *almost entirely nondescript* 8

Grandad cries telling me about his friend who died trying to fly
a fighter plane under the Bristol Suspension Bridge 9

Poem in which I google fighter planes flying under the Bristol
Suspension Bridge 10

Grandad says something beautiful about his first wife
at her funeral 12

Grandad has lied to his live-in carer about whether or not
he likes chocolate 13

Grandad asks me to read the Walt Whitman poem he chose
for his second wife's funeral, in case he cannot 14

Poem in which Mum tells me things I should not know
about him 15

Grandad was almost poached for an Anglican choir but
his dad wouldn't let him because they were Methodists
and they couldn't have the Anglicans taking their
best voices (*conversation transcribed verbatim*)   16

Poem in which we fix a bike together and he tells me not
to touch the chain because I'll get my white t-shirt covered
in oil   18

Poem in which I get my white t-shirt covered in oil   19

Portrait of Grandad asleep while I read him 'Chocolate Cake'
by Michael Rosen but he wakes up in time to laugh
at the punchline   20

Poem in which, slowly, all Christmasses are hosted
at Grandad's house   21

Grandad has a small heart attack on the toilet
on Christmas Day   22

Poem in which I make a Christmas ham waiting for
my parents to get back from the hospital   23

Poem in which my sister and I sit quietly and look out
at his garden   24

Poem in which each of his jumpers smells the same and
irrefutably of him. As if being able to fix any problem
with wood and nails and a hammer had a smell.   26

Sugar loaf

The cats won't stop coming to Llandegfedd reservoir.

The Cardiff Corporation flooded the village of Glascoed in 1965.
They poured the Usk into the valley, submerging the gardens,
the hedgerows, the canted roofs of the farmhouses.

Mum believes that the Welsh water acts like formaldehyde,
that each scuff mark on the magnolia paint has been preserved.

Toasters float above laminate countertops.
Pike and perch weave through bobbing cat flaps.
There are paw prints in the silt.

Grandad ate four scones at the reservoir cafe and gift shop,
forgetting them one by one. He was surprised each time
by the tartness of the raspberry jam, the cool weight of clotted cream.
He often cries when he has to think about the past.

When kittens see their reflections in the millpond stillness,
do they think of their mothers' mothers, drowned there?

These cats stalk along the shore,
bringing small birds of loss to their owners' doorsteps.

Gannets

Gannet was my nickname at primary school.
For hunger. For single mindedness.
For the first time I ate more than my dad at dinner.

Gannet, from the Old English *ganot*,
meaning strong or masculine;
the resistance of flesh against teeth;
the swell of muscles or stomach like landscape.

Gannets are divers, plummeting
thirty meters into the rime-cold
Atlantic, a drop
that would shatter a human body
plunging from the same height.

We are too heavy in our bones.

*

I learned the basics of diving,
arms wide in featherless parody—leaping;
my body knife-sharp and cleaving
the pool water. As if I were gutting
the belly of a descaled fish.

The first time I dived from the high board
my body folded into a meteor, colliding with the pool
as if I meant to empty it, a practical lesson
in the physics of surface tension. The grey-dart beak
of a gannet pierces the surface of the ocean
precisely; I wished to be a seabird,
emerging victorious from the swell,
a struggle of pilchard in my beak.

I twisted in the air, my mum told me, after I had screamed
my way up from the stinging depths of the pool.
The welts were already spreading across my back,
barnacles on the bow of a ship.
From then on I couldn't jump
from the high board. I would climb
the wet stairs in the stink of chlorine,
and stand at its tip, watching the spume
from the previous diver dissipate in a spreading circle.

*

Everywhere I go,
I am always coming home.
Running barefoot on the cobbles,
keeping pace with whipthin friends.
I remember flashing lighthouse glances
at their bodies, wondering if I could stop eating
if I wanted their abs and tight waists enough.

Beaksharp bones burst through
my cheeks when I took up fasting.
Mum and body were worried,
both gurgled, both asked questions.
Wings of ribcage fluttered
when I lifted my shirt. Each one-meal day
felt like a ritual, or a cleansing,
a chlorine solution for the shame
of my pre-growth-spurt body.
I stung with pride when I grew taller than my dad.

*

I want you to touch my stomach.
I dream of your hands on me,
undeterred by my softness,
the seafloor pockmarked with your footprints.

Let's go swimming in all the ways I used to hate myself:
a deep pool of tensed muscles and stomachs
sucked in like coastlines. Like when Sian slipped
her hand under my jumper and it felt like a gutting.
My whole body shook and I could not tell her about
the way shame was darting through me like minnows.

I want to be touched like that now.
I want to be hungry, to be fed.
I want to be descaled by the rough edges of my throat.
I want to dive off the ragged cliff edge of my body.

*

I didn't eat yesterday, as if hunger were a diving board.
Hunger, from the old English *hungor*, meaning desire;
divers surfacing with fistfuls of pearls; famine.
Meaning I feel empty, but in a controlled way.
Meaning I hope things change.

I have loved this body, written poems
in praise of it, done my best to quell
the shore breakers threatening
to dump it onto the sand.

*

I walked onto the beach in winter
and stripped down to my boxers.
The cold raised a flurry of goosebumps
across my shoulder blades.
The wet sand caught my footprints
and let them go.

I swam and swam and swam
until my lungs were sharp coral
in my chest and I twisted up,
emerging from the spume
with a mackerel in my teeth.

I am always coming home.

*

Fish schooled under the prows of gillnetters and beam trawlers
as I prepared to leap from the viewing platform of the lighthouse.
I dangled a foot over the edge of the railings and learned
that my fear of heights is a fear of the body throwing itself from them.

The practice of cliff or pier jumping came to be known as tombstoning,
as if the edge we teeter on is our mortality, not a granite wall or an outcropping
of rock over the rime-cold Atlantic. They employed somebody
to keep watch in the lighthouse, to scare away the jumpers.

Instead, people take tourist boats out to Seal Island,
on the rocks there is sometimes a plunging of gannets.
It is enough, sometimes, to get something other than what you wanted.

Acknowledgements

Thanks to *Abridged, Ambit, And Other Poems*, Bad Betty Press, *Finished Creatures, The Penn Review, Riggwelter Press, Under the Radar, Up the Staircase* and Yaffle Press for publishing earlier versions of some of the poems in this pamphlet.

Thanks, Dad, for being cool about these poems. Thank you to Carol and Holly Lanyon, who have endured years of poetry, from 2003 emo Chris to 2022 emo Chris. Thank you to Joshua Judson, for reading many early iterations of this maritime nonsense. Thank you, Nicola Toon, for making my sea-goth cover dreams a reality. Thanks to Jake and Amy for believing in my sad bird poems. Thanks to the editors who have published me and to the poets who have workshopped, edited, performed, and partied with me. Thank you to my friends from Nottingham, London, Bristol and Cornwall. Thank you to Leanne Toon, whom I love.